Artlist THE DOG

WHY DO DOGS LOVE TO SNIFF?
The Do's and Don'ts of the Dogs

By The Dogs
As told to Howie Dewin

SCHOLASTIC INC.

New York   Toronto   London   Auckland   Sydney
Mexico City   New Delhi   Hong Kong   Buenos Aires

ISBN-10: 0-439-02255-X
ISBN-13: 978-0-439-02255-2

© 2007 Artlist INTERNATIONAL

12 11 10 9 8 7 6 5 4 3 2 1   7 8 9 10 11/0

Printed in the U.S.A.
First printing, February 2007

Let's face it—
the world is full of rules.

You're a kid. We're Dogs.
Who knows more about rules than us?

There are do's and there are don'ts.

The best thing we can do is know the difference. Because when we don't, trouble happens. And it seems like it's usually a kid or a dog who gets blamed.

But don't worry! We Dogs are here to help. We're starting

with the do's and don'ts of taking care of dogs. We've written down every do and don't we know.

Do we Dogs like all of these do's
and don'ts? Well, some dogs do and some dogs don't.

But we still have to live by them.

So, do read this book so you don't make a mistake when it comes to taking care of one of us.

We think it's important.
Don't you?

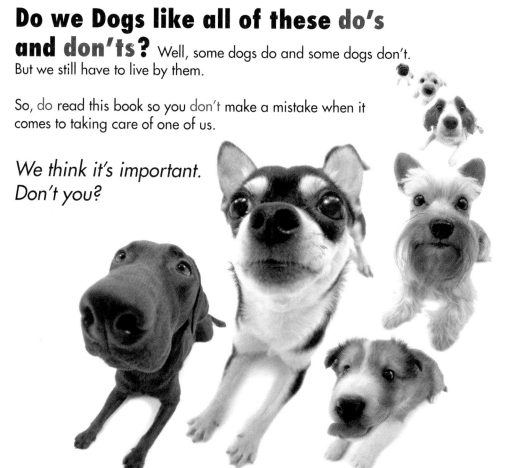

Which Dog Is Perfect for You?

This is important — ALL DOGS ARE DIFFERENT!

Just like people, each of us Dogs likes different things. Each of us does some things well and other things not so well. Each of us needs a different amount of attention.

So get to know us a bit before you adopt us into your family. You can start by learning about different breeds of us Dogs, but that won't tell you everything. After all, is every seven-year-old boy with red hair the same? Is every tall eight-year-old girl like every other tall eight-year-old girl? Of course not!

Those descriptions only tell you a little bit. To really see if that person (or dog) can be your friend, you have to get to know them.

Here are some things you can do to help decide which dog should join your family.

1) Learn about different breeds. Read books and talk to dog owners.

2) Remember our motto: Different Breeds, Different Needs. Ask yourself:

- How much space do we have for a dog?
- Do we have a yard? Is it fenced in?
- Are there other animals in our home?
- How much time can I spend with a dog?

3) Spend time with us one-on-one. Get to know different dogs.

If you want a quiet dog, **DON'T** pick me!

When choosing the right dog for you and your family . . .

DON'T:
. . . choose by color.
. . . just go by description alone.
. . . pick a dog that's too big for your home.
. . . be impatient. Finding the right dog can take time.

DO:
. . . spend time with a dog before adopting it.
. . . find out the dog's history.
. . . be home a lot when your dog is new.
. . . get the dog checked by your vet.

 # Is Your Home Ready for a Dog?

Puppies need homes that are "puppy-proof." Making a home safe and disaster-free for little feet (or paws) takes some thinking.

Having a baby in your home, whether it's human or canine, means there will be some changes. We don't mean to make trouble, but sometimes trouble finds us in homes that haven't been looked at from our point of view.

Here are some things to think about:

DON'T let things break!
Where are fragile things? Are they out of the way of traffic? If they are up high, are they stable? If a piece of furniture gets knocked, will anything fragile fall off?

DO keep food out of reach!
Where is food? Is it up high? Or is it behind a door that closes tightly? Are there any dishes of nuts or candy sitting around? (Chocolate is *really* bad for us.)

If you don't have a high shelf for your good shoes, **DON'T** pick me!

DON'T leave chewable things around if you don't want them chewed!

This is a big one. Until we get used to living with each other, it's hard to know if you're saving that shoe for your foot or if you left it out so we could chew on it. The same goes for your favorite stuffed hedgehog.

DO set limits!

Are there special rooms (or beds) where we aren't supposed to be? Are there doors or gates to help us remember not to go there? (Maybe you could give us our own spot. Sometimes a small space is better in a big scary house. At least until we get to know it!)

> **DO** make sure I have a quiet room. I hide under the couch if it's too loud.

When you are getting ready to bring home a new dog . . .

DON'T:
...buy a brand-new rug.
...bring home a new cat the same week.
...make plans for a family vacation.
...expect things to run smoothly from the start.

DO:
...make sure the yard is fenced in.
...decide where the dog can go and can't go.
...get a leash.
...plan to have fun!

Q: **When Is a Dog**
Doo a Dog Don't?

A: When you're talking about housebreaking.

It's the one time when DON'T is definitely better than DO!

Just like with human babies, potty-training (or housebreaking) takes time and patience. But if you give us clear, consistent information, we will learn to go outside.

There are several ways to teach us "DON'T!"

The most common one involves old newspapers. Lay the sheets of newspaper in a specific place in the house. This teaches the puppy that "taking care of business" happens in a single place . . . not just anywhere in the house. There is a place to DO your business and places where you DON'T.

If you **DON'T** catch me having an accident, **DON'T** punish me for it! (And **DON'T** rub my nose in it.)

If you're going out, **DO** put me in a small sleeping area with no rugs.

There is another way to train a puppy, but it's pretty tiring. It's called "constant supervision." This means someone has to be watching *all the time*. This is possible if someone is home every day. He or she can get to know the puppy's "signs." These are things the puppy does whenever it needs to go to the bathroom. These things might include getting restless, sniffing at old "accident" spots, or just sniffing the floor.

When you're housebreaking your dog . . .

DON'T:

...leave us alone in the house for too long!
...expect miracles. (These things take time.)
...scold us unless you catch us having an accident.
...ask us to use toilet paper.
...take a puppy out to use the bathroom and start to play instead. (It's confusing!)

DO:

...collect plenty of newspapers.
...take us to the same place each time.
...tell us when we've been good.
...be understanding.

DON'T forget the regular times I will always have to go . . . like after I eat or when I wake up.

How Can You Help Us Keep Our Fur Fabulous?

We have one word for you — brushing.

Brushing keeps us looking our silky best. It also helps make sure other problems are not developing. If you brush us often, you will notice if fleas have shown up. You will notice if there are any ticks on us. You'll see for yourself if there are any sores or swelling or other signs of trouble.

Of course, we also will stay beautiful! And you won't have quite so much fur around your house. (Sorry about that shedding business. It's part of what we do!)

But fabulous fur is not just about brushing. It's also about what we eat. A high-protein diet is good for a shiny coat (and good muscles!).

DON'T
forget to brush my beard, too.

THE DON'T BRUSH LIST

Miniature Pinscher
Chihuahua
Smooth-Haired Dachshund

A damp-cloth rubdown is better.

Baths can help, too, but some of us have sensitive skin. Too many baths can cause itchy problems.

That brings us back to brushing. Brushing is really the most important thing. Did we mention brushing?

DON'T bring me to a tropical climate — I have about ten pounds of fur!

SOME BREEDS DON'T SHED!
Yorkshire Terrier
Miniature Schnauzer
Bichon Frise

DO consider powdering me down under my folds when it's hot.

When taking care of our fur . . .

DON'T:
...use your own brush.
...use harsh soaps.
...clip fur without asking your groomer or vet.
...forget the tail. (The longer the tail, the dirtier it gets!)
...be surprised when your dog sheds!

DO:
...brush regularly.
...check for fleas and ticks.
...take your time with tangles. (Ouch!)
...call the groomer if the job is just too big.

Can You Help Keep Our Teeth and Nails Healthy?

We Dogs need to have good teeth to eat, and healthy feet to get around!

So, because it's hard to brush without any thumbs, we need your help with the teeth. The best thing you can do is make sure we have healthy chew toys or snacks. The important thing is that we keep our teeth and gums clean by chewing on something tough.

When you can't ride a bicycle and don't have a skateboard, it's important to keep your feet in good shape. We walk all the time. Our feet and toes and nails have to stay healthy. So please learn how to trim our nails.

Ask our doctor so you can learn about the veins in our nails. You *really* don't want to cut our nails too short. (We really don't want you to, either!)

DON'T be shocked that my tongue is black. It's supposed to be!

DO *give me lots of chew toys and rope toys and balls!*

When taking care of your dog's teeth and nails . . .

DON'T:

. . . share your toothbrush.
. . . ignore bad breath. It's a sign of teeth trouble.
. . . feed your dog only wet food.
. . . skip your dog's veterinary dental visit.

DO:

. . . give your pup rawhide or something harder to chew.
. . . keep your dog's nails clipped, but not too short.
. . . learn how to brush your dog's teeth (with your dog's tooth-brush and toothpaste!)

Do Our Eyes, Ears, and Noses Need Special Attention?

We don't want to brag, but we Dogs have some pretty amazing senses.

We hear ten times better than you. After all, we have twice as many ear muscles!

Our eyes work better in dim light than yours. (We have a layer in our eyes that reflects light. It helps in the dark. It also makes it seem as if our eyes are glowing!)

And let's not even talk about smelling! Well, okay. Let's. You have about 5 million "smelling" cells in your nose. We have as many as 220 million! That's one of the reasons we sniff so much. We're picking up all sorts of yummy smells, all the time! They help us understand everything around us.

But we don't want to show off. In fact, we need your help to keep our eyes and ears and nose healthy. So if you see something funny, don't ignore it.

DO put "clean ears" on your weekly to-do list.

Here are some signs that our eyes, ears, or nose needs attention:

- Black waxy buildup in our ears
- Matted hair around our ears
- Runny, gooey, or crusty eyes
- Winking or squinting or blinking a lot
- Scratching our ears a lot
- "Wiping" our eyes a lot
- Runny nose (just like you!)
- Head shaking or holding our heads at a strange angle
- Red or inflamed skin

Of course, exercise and a good diet are big parts of keeping us healthy all around!

*Please **DON'T** get water in my ears!*

***DON'T** forget that "big lovable eyes" also means "eyes that need attention."*

When you're checking our eyes and ears . . .

DON'T:

. . . expect newborn puppies to see or hear (or smell)!

. . . let our heads hang out car windows (debris, insects, wind—bad for eyes, ears, and nose!)

. . . use out-of-date ointments, creams, or drops (or those not prescribed for your dog).

. . . poke anything into our ears.

DO:

. . . expect grown dogs to see better in the dark than you.

. . . learn simple eye care from your vet.

. . . visit a vet if something like a thorn needs to be removed from your dog's eye.

. . . smell our ears for trouble. If they smell sour, that's not good!

Does It Matter What We Eat?

Does it matter what you eat? Of course it does! It matters what we eat, too.

Some of our rules are the same as yours:

- We shouldn't eat a lot of snacks.
- Candy (especially chocolate) isn't good for us.
- We need plenty of protein.
- We shouldn't eat table scraps. They usually have too much fat.

Some of our rules are different:

- Eat from a bowl on the floor.
- Lick our plates.
- Growl when someone asks for a taste.

DON'T give us chocolate . . . especially baking chocolate.

DON'T IGNORE THESE SIGNS

Overweight
Itchy, flaky skin
Coarse, brittle coat
Low energy
Low resistance to infection

Any of these could be caused by a diet that doesn't have enough protein!

There are a few other things to think about, too. For example, when should you feed your dog? Some of our people feed us at the same time every day. Others leave dry food out so we can nibble when we want. We have different ideas about which is best. Talk to a vet (and your dog) about what works in your home.

Here's another thing to think about. But this one is a secret, so keep it quiet! The leader of the pack always eats first. So, if your dog is around when you eat, you should eat first. Feed your dog second. That shows that you are in charge!

When you're feeding your dog . . .

DON'T:

. . . let canned food sit out more than a half hour before eating.
. . . feed us too much!
. . . forget the meat!
. . . leave the kibbles on a low shelf in an open closet.

DO:

. . . ask your vet to help you create the best diet for your dog.
. . . clean our bowls after every meal.
. . . include dry food in your dog's diet.
. . . make sure our diet is balanced and includes grains.

DO give me lots of protein. I'm an athlete!

How Can You Get Us to Obey?

Let's see . . . *hmmm* . . . how do we say this nicely? We would prefer to focus on good communication rather than that pesky "obey" word.

It's important that you and your dog learn how to understand each other. That way you can both give each other what you both want.

DON'T *expect me **not** to protect my family!*

DO *give me rules. I live to please.*

For example, you will be happy if we don't go to the bathroom on the rug, bark for 35 minutes at four A.M., or dig a hole that makes the right side of the house tilt.

We will be happier if there aren't lots of loud children pulling our tails, or if we don't have to wait too long for dinner.

We need to teach each other!

Let's at least set a few ground rules:

- Obedience training should be fun.
- It should include rewards.
- Sessions should be short.
- Trainers should be patient.
- Start training at home; later, try different locations.

DON'T yell at me if you want me to obey. I get nervous around yelling!

When you're teaching your dog commands . . .

DON'T:
. . . expect us not to be dogs. We'll always drool or howl!
. . . ask a terrier not to dig.
. . . hit your dog.
. . . give up.

DO:
. . . be consistent.
. . . use rewards.
. . . be patient.
. . . use words and signals.
. . . learn about your breed of dog. (Some of us are better at obedience than others!)

How Do You Teach an Old Dog (or Any Dog) a New Trick?

With enough time, patience, and treats, you can teach any dog anything!

Here are some basic hints to get you started.

If you really want us to learn a trick, DO:

- Spend 10 or 20 minutes on tricks every day.
- Teach only one trick at a time. (Otherwise, we might jump up when you say "roll over.")
- Have fun between exercises.
- Start with the basics before moving on to more advanced tricks.
- Make sure your dog looks you in the eye when you say his/her name.

I DON'T want to brag, but I fetch naturally. (I can even fetch a sheep.)

I DO want to DO tricks, but I DON'T want to stop sniffing, so it doesn't usually work out.

The Basics – you and your dog should master these tricks first:

- Take treats (without nipping)
- Hand track (follow your hand when you move it back and forth)
- Name response
- Sit
- Down
- Stand

Then give these a try:

- Bow
- Hop
- High five
- Roll over
- Shake
- Spin

*If you want a smart dog with a history of circus tricks, **DO** pick me!*

When you're teaching your dog a trick . . .

DON'T:

. . . yell

. . . let us get bored.

. . . ask a Yorkie to catch a Frisbee or an Afghan to do a flip.

. . . skip the basics.

DO:

. . . make it like a game with rewards and praise.

. . . understand your dog's natural strengths.

. . . be patient and consistent.

. . . take play breaks between each trick you practice.

Do All Dogs Need Exercise?

Yes! But we're all different. Some breeds need to run and run. Other breeds just need to get off the couch once a day!

Here's what exercise can do: Make healthy bones and joints, make the heart and lungs work better, make dogs look better and feel better!

But that doesn't mean we need to run a marathon every day! Lots of people think dogs don't have any limits. (That's why some of us hurt our legs and knees by jumping too high and running too far.)

Here's what you *don't* want exercise to do: Create injuries, lead to heat exhaustion or heat stroke (we're not very good at cooling ourselves off), or make your dog hyper instead of more relaxed!

This is really a case of getting to know your dog and figuring out what works best.

And remember, this is another way we're just like you — a fun game is a lot better than "exercise"! So how about just grabbing a tennis ball, and we'll toss it around for a while?

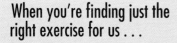

DO *help me be careful not to strain my back.*

When you're finding just the right exercise for us . . .

DON'T:
. . . *try jump roping.*
. . . *let us near the road.*
. . . *put us on a trampoline.*
. . . *ask us to jog with the cat.*

DO:
. . . *make sure the yard is fenced in.*
. . . *know the limits of your dog. (Not everybody was born to run!)*
. . . *keep us on a leash when we're not in the yard.*

Do Dogs Need Friends?

We Dogs are pack animals. That means we usually like to be around other dogs. Of course (as we know), every dog is different. But generally, dogs like dogs.

The big thing about making friends is figuring out who is in charge. We're really good at making that clear right away. We do that by using our tails and noses and ears and voices. But we get better at that kind of thing if we're around other dogs a lot.

It's important to introduce your dog to other dogs from the very start. Make sure your puppy meets other dogs (and people and cats and anyone else you want your dog to like). Look for a park or playground near you where other dogs and their families spend time.

DO introduce me around. I like everyone . . . even horses!

No offense, but playing with another dog is the best thing there is. You are our best friends, but you only have two legs and you just don't run fast enough!

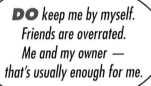

> **DON'T** keep me away from other dogs. I need my pack!

> **DO** keep me by myself. Friends are overrated. Me and my owner — that's usually enough for me.

When you're introducing your dog to new friends . . .

DON'T:
. . .rush things.
. . .pet a dog you don't know.
. . .assume "little" means "sweet."
. . .leave any dog alone too much.

DO:
. . .start introductions when your dog is a puppy.
. . .keep everyone on leashes until you're certain there won't be trouble.
. . ."read" a dog's signs — tail, growl, ears.
. . .reassure your dog.

How Do You Choose the Right Vet for Us?

Even we Dogs know that when you want to make a smart decision, there are certain things you should always do. You have to learn about the people and places near you that offer what you need. Research your choices.

So, if you're looking for just the right veterinarian, here are the things you need to do:

🐾 Figure out exactly what your dog needs. Does your breed have certain health issues that will need a lot of attention or a special kind of care?

🐾 Find out which veterinarians, animal clinics, or hospitals are near your home.

🐾 Talk to other dog owners about their experiences with vets in your area.

🐾 Schedule a visit to different vet offices. Take a full tour. See what you think. How does the place look, smell, and feel? Does the office have emergency hours and services?

🐾 Meet the doctor. Find out how many other vets work in the same office.

DO choose a vet who recognizes royalty when it's in the room.

Before we wrap up this section, we have one favor to ask — the worst time to look for a vet is when we really need one. So please plan ahead. Choose our vet before an emergency chooses one for us!

DO think of our vet as our **second** best friend, and choose carefully!

When making a visit to your vet . . .

DON'T:

. . . arrive late.

. . . skip annual checkups.

. . . postpone or ignore yearly vaccinations.

. . . expect anyone to diagnose a problem over the phone.

. . . delay if your dog is having a problem.

DO:

. . . learn to recognize "normal" in your dog so you can spot when something's wrong.

. . . arrive at the vet with us on a leash!

. . . call ahead in an emergency. (We might need to go elsewhere if the vet isn't available! It's always good to know where the nearest animal emergency clinic is located, as a backup.)

. . . post our vet's number somewhere handy in case of an emergency.

Do You Have to Worry About Fleas, Ticks, and Other Pests?

Yes! Please!

Okay. Maybe you don't have to *worry*. But it would be good if you would check us often to make sure we don't have any. Remember, you can catch them, too, so you don't want to mess around with these critters!

Springtime is the worst time for fleas, ticks, flies, and other creeps. They love the moisture and heat. (But that doesn't mean they can't show up other times, so always be on the lookout.) If fleas get in the house, then anything can happen, because houses stay warm all the time.

> **DON'T** ignore our signs — scratching, skin bumps, biting around our tail and thighs, and black specks of flea dirt that turn red on a wet paper towel. Gross!

FLEA FACTS
- Fleas live for 50 days.
- A female can lay more than 2,000 eggs in 50 days.
- Fleas can jump 100 times their height.

The best thing we can suggest is to help us stay free of the little pests with good care and grooming. There are also lots of different products you can buy to help keep us flea and tick free. (And it doesn't always mean strong chemicals!)

The best approach will depend on your situation. Do you live in a place where fleas and ticks are a big problem or not such a big problem? Is your dog infested? Is your house infested? All these questions will help you and your vet decide the best solution.

But here's one thing everyone should know — don't ignore these little guys. They may be small, but they're fierce!

DON'T let a tick confuse me with a taxi. I don't pick up passengers!

If you're trying to keep pests off your pet . . .

DON'T:

. . .expect to see the actual pest — look for the signs instead.
. . .skip a treatment if you're on a monthly program.
. . .ignore sickness after removal of a tick. (See the vet.)
. . .go for walks in marshy or tall-grass areas.

DO:

. . .brush and examine your dog's fur on a regular basis.
. . .learn about the different products that help control pests.
. . .keep your lawn clear of tall grass, and control shrubs.
. . .remove embedded ticks right away.

Does a Dog Need Stuff?

Here's another thing we have in common — chances are we don't need half the stuff we have. But that doesn't mean a little stuff isn't fun.

Here are the things we DO need:

- Collar
- Leash
- Food bowl (with food)
- Water bowl (with water)
- Safe play area
- Pest control
- Veterinary care

Here are things *some of us* need:

- Sweater
- Brush
- Grooming
- Muzzle

*I **DON'T** want a sweater, I **need** a sweater, thank you very much.*

MORE STUFF DOGS DON'T NEED

Lipstick
Fork
Jeans
Driver's license
Piano lessons
Tree house

Here are things we DON'T need (but might enjoy!):

- 🐾 Dog stroller
- 🐾 Lunch box
- 🐾 Canopy bed
- 🐾 Furniture
- 🐾 Cookies
- 🐾 Diamond-studded anything
- 🐾 Birthday parties

> *I **DON'T** consider a brush an optional item.*

> *I **DO** enjoy a really pretty, bouncy, expensive doggy ball. But I also really enjoy a good stick. Feel free to give me either.*

When shopping for your dog . . .

DON'T:
. . . *spend more on clothes than food.*
. . . *think it's necessary to have fancy toys.*
. . . *overdo treats.*
. . . *torment your dog with too much dress-up.*

DO:
. . . *think about whether your dog will like it as much as you do.*
. . . *spend more time playing with your dog than shopping for your dog.*
. . . *choose toys that will encourage appropriate exercise.*
. . . *make it clear to your dog what are dog toys and what are people toys.*

THE BIG DON'T:
Abuse and Neglect

THE BIG DO:
Love and Respect

Who knows dogs better than us?

Like it or not, the world is full of **do's** and **don'ts**. We Dogs think it's a good idea to know the difference! And, because we're your best pals, it's only fair that we share what we've learned.

We're starting with the do's and don'ts of caring for your favorite pooches. After all, we're experts! Here, we bark about how to choose the perfect pup for you, how to keep our fur fabulous, an how to understand the silly things we do.

So, whatever you **do, don't** miss all of the great tips inside!

GO TO

This edition is only available for distribution through the school market.

ISBN-13: 978-0-439-022
ISBN-10: 0-439-02255-X

EAN

9 780439 022552

MATT
SHAW

THE
SUICIDE
CLUB